# I brushed my hair today

## A MOM JOURNAL

for Mostly Together Moms

By

KAREN JOHNSON

Illustrations by Chelsea Larsson

ROCKRIDGE
PRESS

# INTRODUCTION

## Hey, mama.

You're exhausted and have a gajillion things on your to-do list, and now someone has handed you a journal to write in. WTF, right? But this one's different, I promise.

This journal is for writing about the truth of being a mom—the happy days, the rough days, and everything in between. And yes, for venting about how sometimes your kids are jerks. This doesn't mean you don't love them and know that you're #blessed to be their mommy. Because of course you do.

But this shit is hard, isn't it? In many ways, motherhood is probably exactly what you thought it would be, and, in some ways, you're like umm . . . is this really what I signed up for? So, don't jot down the cute stuff or the sweet stuff or the "baby's first" milestones in here (unless you want to). Save the sugary sappiness for the *Winnie the Pooh* Mommy-and-Me book your Aunt Cathy gave you.

*This* journal is for writing about how your oh-so-adorable child peed through her clothes while throwing eggs out of the cart at Target. *This* journal is for admitting that after that episode, you not-so-quietly muttered "fucking SHIT," and went home to drink wine during naptime.

*This* journal is without judgment, and it was created by a mom who has been there. A mom who has wiped poop off the walls five minutes before company walked in the door, who has caught vomit from one kid after breastfeeding another for the third time in the middle of the night, and who tossed Skittles into her last kid's mouth while he pooped because she was desperate to get him finally potty-trained and bid farewell to diapers forever.

As someone who has cried into her coffee about how damn hard this motherhood journey is, I know one thing for sure: We moms need a place to tell our unvarnished stories. This journal's

daily writing space and weekly prompts allow you to record a year's worth of the crappiest (literally or figuratively), funniest, most exhausting, and most rewarding parenting moments. And, bonus—there's also an "inspirational" quote from other moms, so you know you're not on this journey alone. Before you even know it, you'll have survived a year of motherhood, having kept it mostly together, and you can look back on how much you've grown, how much being a mom has changed you (for the good and bad), and how many cookies you consumed to cope.

I hope these pages make you laugh, feel less alone, and help you purge some frustrations after a long day of negotiating with tiny terrorists who make you an hour late for everything because they can put on their shoes "all by myself!"

And from one mama to another, let me say this final truth: You got this.

—KAREN JOHNSON,
a mostly together mom of three

I've conquered a lot of things...blood clots in my lungs—twice...knee and foot surgeries... winning Grand Slams being down match point...to name just a few, but I found out by far the hardest is figuring out a stroller!

—SERENA WILLIAMS, professional tennis player and entrepreneur

MONTH | DAY | YEAR

MONTH | DAY | YEAR

MONTH | DAY | YEAR

MONTH | DAY | YEAR

MONTH | DAY | YEAR

MONTH | DAY | YEAR

MONTH | DAY | YEAR

*Parenting is full of surprises. Some moments are joyous—like your baby's first laugh, and some are awful—like when your toddler finds a Sharpie. What has been the biggest shock of parenting for you so far?*

What are the tell-tale signs that your personal standards are officially in the toilet? Is it your "outfit" of a sweatshirt from college and leggings with holes in the crotch?

You know you've grown a lot as a parent when you watch your kid lick something in public and you think: "Eh. He's licked worse."

—MEREDITH ETHINGTON, writer and creator of Perfection Pending

MONTH | DAY | YEAR

...........................................................................................................

...........................................................................................................

MONTH | DAY | YEAR

...........................................................................................................

...........................................................................................................

MONTH | DAY | YEAR

...........................................................................................................

...........................................................................................................

MONTH | DAY | YEAR

...........................................................................................................

...........................................................................................................

MONTH | DAY | YEAR

...........................................................................................................

...........................................................................................................

MONTH | DAY | YEAR

...........................................................................................................

...........................................................................................................

MONTH | DAY | YEAR

...........................................................................................................

...........................................................................................................

...........................................................................................................

MONTH | DAY | YEAR

MONTH | DAY | YEAR

MONTH | DAY | YEAR

MONTH | DAY | YEAR

MONTH | DAY | YEAR

MONTH | DAY | YEAR

MONTH | DAY | YEAR

*It's been five minutes, and no one has climbed on you, asked to be wiped, or demanded a snack. OMG, it has happened: The kids are quiet! What do you do?*

If your toddler is quiet for a very long time, your Christmas tree is now just a regular tree.

—JOELLE WISLER, writer

*How are you retaining the few brain cells you have left (or have you given up entirely)?*

My friends make me feel dumb now. They're talking about Syria and Egypt, and I'm just, like, "Oscar was out of control on Sesame Street. He was extra-grouchy today."

—WANDA SYKES,
actress and comedian

MONTH | DAY | YEAR

..............................................................................................

..............................................................................................

MONTH | DAY | YEAR

..............................................................................................

..............................................................................................

MONTH | DAY | YEAR

..............................................................................................

..............................................................................................

MONTH | DAY | YEAR

..............................................................................................

..............................................................................................

MONTH | DAY | YEAR

..............................................................................................

..............................................................................................

MONTH | DAY | YEAR

..............................................................................................

..............................................................................................

MONTH | DAY | YEAR

..............................................................................................

..............................................................................................

..............................................................................................

MONTH | DAY | YEAR

MONTH | DAY | YEAR

MONTH | DAY | YEAR

MONTH | DAY | YEAR

MONTH | DAY | YEAR

MONTH | DAY | YEAR

MONTH | DAY | YEAR

Meditation is my thing. But I'm not going to lie. Sometimes I get into my closet and lock the door so no one can find me.

—GWEN STEFANI, musician

*When you need five minutes to yourself, where do you hide from your kids? And when they find you, where do you hide next?*

In the age of social media, when you can edit your life in beautiful pictures, it's important to remind moms that all of us are wearing yogurt and all of our hands smell like urine.

—KRISTEN BELL, actress

MONTH | DAY | YEAR

MONTH | DAY | YEAR

MONTH | DAY | YEAR

MONTH | DAY | YEAR

MONTH | DAY | YEAR

MONTH | DAY | YEAR

MONTH | DAY | YEAR

Today's Special
MAMMA
MASSAGE

*What does mom's night out look like these days? Is it getting ready with a toddler clinging to your leg while you're trying to pump? Or is going out just a mere fantasy right now?*

*A sanctimommy judged your parenting on social media. How did you respond to her comments in your head (f-bombs, obviously), and how did you respond for real?*

Welcome to parenthood. For the next 18 years, everything you do will be wrong to someone, somewhere.

—LAUREN LODDER, writer and creator of *Mommy Owl*

MONTH | DAY | YEAR

...................................................................................................................

...................................................................................................................

MONTH | DAY | YEAR

...................................................................................................................

...................................................................................................................

MONTH | DAY | YEAR

...................................................................................................................

...................................................................................................................

MONTH | DAY | YEAR

...................................................................................................................

...................................................................................................................

MONTH | DAY | YEAR

...................................................................................................................

...................................................................................................................

MONTH | DAY | YEAR

...................................................................................................................

...................................................................................................................

MONTH | DAY | YEAR

...................................................................................................................

...................................................................................................................

MONTH | DAY | YEAR

MONTH | DAY | YEAR

MONTH | DAY | YEAR

MONTH | DAY | YEAR

MONTH | DAY | YEAR

MONTH | DAY | YEAR

MONTH | DAY | YEAR

*Confession time! What's something you swore you'd never do when you had kids that you're now totally guilty of? (No judgment if it's "Let them watch hours of TV and eat fruit snacks on the couch.")*

Mentally preparing for 13-hour travel day with toddler. My suitcase is mostly full of bribes.

—OLIVIA WILDE, actress

All my friends are posting photos of their exotic beach vacations on Facebook, and I'm over here in the dark listening to the sound of ocean waves on my kids' white noise machine.

—CANDACE ALNAJI, attorney and writer for *Her View from Home*

MONTH | DAY | YEAR

........................................................................................................

........................................................................................................

MONTH | DAY | YEAR

........................................................................................................

........................................................................................................

MONTH | DAY | YEAR

........................................................................................................

........................................................................................................

MONTH | DAY | YEAR

........................................................................................................

........................................................................................................

MONTH | DAY | YEAR

........................................................................................................

........................................................................................................

MONTH | DAY | YEAR

........................................................................................................

........................................................................................................

MONTH | DAY | YEAR

........................................................................................................

........................................................................................................

........................................................................................................

MONTH | DAY | YEAR

........................................................................................................................................

........................................................................................................................................

MONTH | DAY | YEAR

........................................................................................................................................

........................................................................................................................................

MONTH | DAY | YEAR

........................................................................................................................................

........................................................................................................................................

MONTH | DAY | YEAR

........................................................................................................................................

........................................................................................................................................

MONTH | DAY | YEAR

........................................................................................................................................

........................................................................................................................................

MONTH | DAY | YEAR

........................................................................................................................................

........................................................................................................................................

MONTH | DAY | YEAR

........................................................................................................................................

........................................................................................................................................

........................................................................................................................................

My three-year-old could not say the "st" sound yet—it sounded like a "d." So you can imagine what happened when he found a huge stick and ran around the neighborhood telling everyone how big his "stick" was.

—ME, a mortified mom of three

Apparently you have to get the baby to latch on at a very specific angle. You gotta tilt their head and do geometry to get them on properly. And it's very stressful because when they're hungry and they're crying it makes your hormones spray milk all over their face and their neck, which then becomes very slippery and hard to grip, and then you gotta slam them on at just the right time, and every time I would do it, it was like parallel parking: I don't know how I did it!

—ALI WONG, comedian

MONTH | DAY | YEAR

MONTH | DAY | YEAR

MONTH | DAY | YEAR

MONTH | DAY | YEAR

MONTH | DAY | YEAR

MONTH | DAY | YEAR

MONTH | DAY | YEAR

*What is something that you thought would be easier but is actually gut-wrenchingly, punch-you-in-the-face, make-you-want-to-day-drink hard?*

Sign your kids up for sports so you can spend $150 per season to watch them sit in the middle of a field and cry.

—LAURA, writer and creator of Sammiches and Psych Meds

MONTH | DAY | YEAR

...............................................................................................................

...............................................................................................................

MONTH | DAY | YEAR

...............................................................................................................

...............................................................................................................

MONTH | DAY | YEAR

...............................................................................................................

...............................................................................................................

MONTH | DAY | YEAR

...............................................................................................................

...............................................................................................................

MONTH | DAY | YEAR

...............................................................................................................

...............................................................................................................

MONTH | DAY | YEAR

...............................................................................................................

...............................................................................................................

MONTH | DAY | YEAR

...............................................................................................................

...............................................................................................................

...............................................................................................................

MONTH | DAY | YEAR

MONTH | DAY | YEAR

MONTH | DAY | YEAR

MONTH | DAY | YEAR

MONTH | DAY | YEAR

MONTH | DAY | YEAR

MONTH | DAY | YEAR

Remember the days of owning break-able vases and having walls that were "undecorated" with crayon? What do you miss most about your house before kids?

I cleaned the floors yesterday. According to my kids, that makes today "Let's Spill All the Sticky and Crumby Things on the Floor Day."

— AMBER LEVENTRY, writer and creator of Family Rhetoric by Amber Leventry

*From counting your child's poops to calculating the ratio of chicken nuggets consumed to chicken nuggets thrown on the floor—no one tells you how much math you'll use in motherhood. How have you used it this week?*

It just occurred to me that the majority of my diet is made up of the foods that my kid didn't finish.

—CARRIE UNDERWOOD, musician

MONTH | DAY | YEAR

MONTH | DAY | YEAR

MONTH | DAY | YEAR

MONTH | DAY | YEAR

MONTH | DAY | YEAR

MONTH | DAY | YEAR

MONTH | DAY | YEAR

MONTH | DAY | YEAR

MONTH | DAY | YEAR

MONTH | DAY | YEAR

MONTH | DAY | YEAR

MONTH | DAY | YEAR

MONTH | DAY | YEAR

MONTH | DAY | YEAR

Hi, my daughter will be late to school because she can zip her jacket all by herself.

—JULIE BURTON, writer

Milestones are important for your kids, but moms deserve praise too. This shit is hard! What #momwin did you have this week? (Maybe you cut a poop-filled onesie off of your baby for the first time. Yay, milestone.)

If I wasn't at work, I just wanted to stay home and party with my little man—and by "party" I mean, of course, endless rounds of Itsy Bitsy Spider.

—OLIVIA WILDE, actress

MONTH | DAY | YEAR

.........................................................................................................................

.........................................................................................................................

MONTH | DAY | YEAR

.........................................................................................................................

.........................................................................................................................

MONTH | DAY | YEAR

.........................................................................................................................

.........................................................................................................................

MONTH | DAY | YEAR

.........................................................................................................................

.........................................................................................................................

MONTH | DAY | YEAR

.........................................................................................................................

.........................................................................................................................

MONTH | DAY | YEAR

.........................................................................................................................

.........................................................................................................................

MONTH | DAY | YEAR

.........................................................................................................................

.........................................................................................................................

.........................................................................................................................

*How has mundane repetition ruined your life lately?*

I never realized you could say "I love you too" with an undercurrent of rage. But then I birthed manipulative toddlers who don't like to eat dinner.

—BECCA CARNAHAN, writer and creator of *With Love, Becca*

MONTH | DAY | YEAR

......................................................................................................

......................................................................................................

MONTH | DAY | YEAR

......................................................................................................

......................................................................................................

MONTH | DAY | YEAR

......................................................................................................

......................................................................................................

MONTH | DAY | YEAR

......................................................................................................

......................................................................................................

MONTH | DAY | YEAR

......................................................................................................

......................................................................................................

MONTH | DAY | YEAR

......................................................................................................

......................................................................................................

MONTH | DAY | YEAR

......................................................................................................

......................................................................................................

......................................................................................................

MONTH | DAY | YEAR

MONTH | DAY | YEAR

MONTH | DAY | YEAR

MONTH | DAY | YEAR

MONTH | DAY | YEAR

MONTH | DAY | YEAR

MONTH | DAY | YEAR

*Time to hand out an award! And "The Asshole of the Week" goes to:*

I am having a very rough day and it would help me a lot if any moms would like to share stories of their kids being mean to them.

—CHRISSY TEIGEN,
model and author

OMG IF I HAVE TO READ BROWN BEAR, BROWN BEAR AGAIN
MY HEAD WILL EXPLODE. What's the most frustrating
part of the bedtime routine with your sweet cherub?

My son just offered to do the laundry
so he could get out of bedtime. What
an interesting conundrum.

—KRISTEN CHASE, Publisher and
CEO of Cool Mom Picks

MONTH | DAY | YEAR

........................................................................................

........................................................................................

MONTH | DAY | YEAR

........................................................................................

........................................................................................

MONTH | DAY | YEAR

........................................................................................

........................................................................................

MONTH | DAY | YEAR

........................................................................................

........................................................................................

MONTH | DAY | YEAR

........................................................................................

........................................................................................

MONTH | DAY | YEAR

........................................................................................

........................................................................................

MONTH | DAY | YEAR

........................................................................................

........................................................................................

........................................................................................

MONTH | DAY | YEAR

.....................................................................................................................................................

.....................................................................................................................................................

MONTH | DAY | YEAR

.....................................................................................................................................................

.....................................................................................................................................................

MONTH | DAY | YEAR

.....................................................................................................................................................

.....................................................................................................................................................

MONTH | DAY | YEAR

.....................................................................................................................................................

.....................................................................................................................................................

MONTH | DAY | YEAR

.....................................................................................................................................................

.....................................................................................................................................................

MONTH | DAY | YEAR

.....................................................................................................................................................

.....................................................................................................................................................

MONTH | DAY | YEAR

.....................................................................................................................................................

.....................................................................................................................................................

.....................................................................................................................................................

I turn activewear into just wear.

—SERENA DORMAN, writer
and creator of *Mommy Cusses*

I'm exhausted this
week because:

Having kids is like hiring an interior decorator just to [mess] up your house... "Do you have any applesauce or mint jelly? I need to put that in your cushions."

—WANDA SYKES, actress and comedian

MONTH | DAY | YEAR

MONTH | DAY | YEAR

MONTH | DAY | YEAR

MONTH | DAY | YEAR

MONTH | DAY | YEAR

MONTH | DAY | YEAR

MONTH | DAY | YEAR

Your doorbell rings. It's your neighbor whose house is straight out of a Pottery Barn catalog. Your living room looks like it has been trampled through by rampaging dinosaurs. What do you do?

It all started at 5:30 am, when the threenager woke up too early. She has been ill and wanted to color. And that's when the first battle began—before the sun was up and before I'd had coffee. OVER CRAYONS.

—KRISTEN HEWITT, *Scary Mommy writer*

MONTH | DAY | YEAR

..........................................................................................................

..........................................................................................................

MONTH | DAY | YEAR

..........................................................................................................

..........................................................................................................

MONTH | DAY | YEAR

..........................................................................................................

..........................................................................................................

MONTH | DAY | YEAR

..........................................................................................................

..........................................................................................................

MONTH | DAY | YEAR

..........................................................................................................

..........................................................................................................

MONTH | DAY | YEAR

..........................................................................................................

..........................................................................................................

MONTH | DAY | YEAR

..........................................................................................................

..........................................................................................................

..........................................................................................................

MONTH | DAY | YEAR

.......................................................................................................................

.......................................................................................................................

MONTH | DAY | YEAR

.......................................................................................................................

.......................................................................................................................

MONTH | DAY | YEAR

.......................................................................................................................

.......................................................................................................................

MONTH | DAY | YEAR

.......................................................................................................................

.......................................................................................................................

MONTH | DAY | YEAR

.......................................................................................................................

.......................................................................................................................

MONTH | DAY | YEAR

.......................................................................................................................

.......................................................................................................................

MONTH | DAY | YEAR

.......................................................................................................................

.......................................................................................................................

.......................................................................................................................

*What's a recent memorable poop or pee moment? Did your child finally get over their fear of the automatic flush? Or loudly announce in public that poop fell out of their butt?*

Usually the triumph of my day is, you know, everybody making it to the potty.

—JULIA ROBERTS, actress

Ah, babies! They're more than just adorable little creatures on whom you can blame your farts.

—TINA FEY, actress and comedian

MONTH | DAY | YEAR

MONTH | DAY | YEAR

MONTH | DAY | YEAR

MONTH | DAY | YEAR

MONTH | DAY | YEAR

MONTH | DAY | YEAR

MONTH | DAY | YEAR

MONTH | DAY | YEAR

MONTH | DAY | YEAR

MONTH | DAY | YEAR

MONTH | DAY | YEAR

MONTH | DAY | YEAR

MONTH | DAY | YEAR

MONTH | DAY | YEAR

I feel like moms who do wanna feel sexy can be. I don't feel like once you become a mom, you supposed to be this nun.

—CARDI B, musician

How are you getting your groove back?

You get no 401K, no co-workers, you're just in solitary confinement all day long with this human Tamagotchi that doesn't have a reset button, so the stakes are extremely high.

—ALI WONG, comedian

MONTH | DAY | YEAR

MONTH | DAY | YEAR

MONTH | DAY | YEAR

MONTH | DAY | YEAR

MONTH | DAY | YEAR

MONTH | DAY | YEAR

MONTH | DAY | YEAR

Taking a shower and shaving both legs. Eating while breastfeeding and not dropping a single crumb on your baby. What is one thing you accomplished this week?

If by "plans" you mean waiting by the door while my three-year-old puts on his shoes all by himself, then yeah, I've got big plans today.

—ME, still in the driveway, five days later

MONTH | DAY | YEAR

........................................................................................................................

........................................................................................................................

MONTH | DAY | YEAR

........................................................................................................................

........................................................................................................................

MONTH | DAY | YEAR

........................................................................................................................

........................................................................................................................

MONTH | DAY | YEAR

........................................................................................................................

........................................................................................................................

MONTH | DAY | YEAR

........................................................................................................................

........................................................................................................................

MONTH | DAY | YEAR

........................................................................................................................

........................................................................................................................

MONTH | DAY | YEAR

........................................................................................................................

........................................................................................................................

........................................................................................................................

MONTH | DAY | YEAR

························································································

····································································································

MONTH | DAY | YEAR

························································································

····································································································

MONTH | DAY | YEAR

························································································

····································································································

MONTH | DAY | YEAR

························································································

····································································································

MONTH | DAY | YEAR

························································································

····································································································

MONTH | DAY | YEAR

························································································

····································································································

MONTH | DAY | YEAR

························································································

····································································································

····································································································

*What's one parenting "rule" that you used to follow but abandoned completely because you're too damn tired?*

I'm going to write a parenting book called Fine. Whatever. Go Ahead.

—YELISA SWAIN,
writer and creator of
Mother Playlist

*How do you tune out your kids? (C'mon we all do it. They'll be FINE.)*

Yeah my kid [Willow] rides her bike inside. Without clothes. And helmets. While I ignore her and look at my phone.

—PINK, musician

MONTH | DAY | YEAR

MONTH | DAY | YEAR

MONTH | DAY | YEAR

MONTH | DAY | YEAR

MONTH | DAY | YEAR

MONTH | DAY | YEAR

MONTH | DAY | YEAR

MONTH | DAY | YEAR

..................................................................................................................................................

..................................................................................................................................................

MONTH | DAY | YEAR

..................................................................................................................................................

..................................................................................................................................................

MONTH | DAY | YEAR

..................................................................................................................................................

..................................................................................................................................................

MONTH | DAY | YEAR

..................................................................................................................................................

..................................................................................................................................................

MONTH | DAY | YEAR

..................................................................................................................................................

..................................................................................................................................................

MONTH | DAY | YEAR

..................................................................................................................................................

..................................................................................................................................................

MONTH | DAY | YEAR

..................................................................................................................................................

..................................................................................................................................................

My kid has a lot of opinions for someone who rarely wears pants.

—KATEY DISTEFANO, writer and creator of *The Mother Octopus*

*Describe a moment your child was being a total shit but also so effing adorable that you couldn't even be mad.*

Sometimes I forget where I'm driving them to. That happens, right? I don't crash the car, but I do just stop in the middle of the road and go, "Where are we going?" That happens a lot... "How are we in this car, and who am I dropping off, and where are we going?"

—AMY POEHLER, actress and comedian

MONTH | DAY | YEAR

MONTH | DAY | YEAR

MONTH | DAY | YEAR

MONTH | DAY | YEAR

MONTH | DAY | YEAR

MONTH | DAY | YEAR

MONTH | DAY | YEAR

*What did you forget this week?*

Me, at 8 am: "Oh, juice spill? That's okay, kids. Love you."
Me, at 5 pm: "IF ONE MORE GODDAMN DROP OF JUICE spills, I'm burning the house down!"

—STEPHANIE ORTIZ, writer and creator of Six Pack Mom

How many different "mommy personalities" appear in your house over the course of the day? What usually causes a new "mommy" to emerge?

MONTH | DAY | YEAR

MONTH | DAY | YEAR

MONTH | DAY | YEAR

MONTH | DAY | YEAR

MONTH | DAY | YEAR

MONTH | DAY | YEAR

MONTH | DAY | YEAR

MONTH | DAY | YEAR

MONTH | DAY | YEAR

MONTH | DAY | YEAR

MONTH | DAY | YEAR

MONTH | DAY | YEAR

MONTH | DAY | YEAR

MONTH | DAY | YEAR

Your children are always listening. So remember: Use profanity correctly and in the proper context.

—KATHRYN LEEHANE, writer and creator of *Foxy Wine Pocket*

*Is there a place where you can never, ever show your face again because of something your child did?*

Children are like crazy, drunken small people in your house.

—JULIE BOWEN, actress

MONTH | DAY | YEAR

..................................................................................................

..................................................................................................

MONTH | DAY | YEAR

..................................................................................................

..................................................................................................

MONTH | DAY | YEAR

..................................................................................................

..................................................................................................

MONTH | DAY | YEAR

..................................................................................................

..................................................................................................

MONTH | DAY | YEAR

..................................................................................................

..................................................................................................

MONTH | DAY | YEAR

..................................................................................................

..................................................................................................

MONTH | DAY | YEAR

..................................................................................................

..................................................................................................

MONTH | DAY | YEAR

MONTH | DAY | YEAR

MONTH | DAY | YEAR

MONTH | DAY | YEAR

MONTH | DAY | YEAR

MONTH | DAY | YEAR

MONTH | DAY | YEAR

"I'm sorry, no, I don't take orders from people 1/3 my size," I say as I hand over a plate of perfectly cooled cheese toast for the first, cubed pears in the green cup for the second, and fling the third a candy cane because my ears will scream if I hear him ask one more damn time.

—MACGILL MOORE FRUTCHEY, writer and creator of Macgyvering Mom

Dinner is a shitshow because the blue PAW PATROL plate is MIA. What is the craziest, super-particular thing your child HAS to have or do?

I don't love motherhood.
Not every day.
Not every moment.
Not always.

But I do love motherhood.
Not every day.
Not every moment.
Not always.

And that is okay.

—KATIE WEBER, writer and founder
of *Lovely in the Dark*

MONTH | DAY | YEAR

.......................................................................................................................................

...........................................................................................................................................

MONTH | DAY | YEAR

.......................................................................................................................................

...........................................................................................................................................

MONTH | DAY | YEAR

.......................................................................................................................................

...........................................................................................................................................

MONTH | DAY | YEAR

.......................................................................................................................................

...........................................................................................................................................

MONTH | DAY | YEAR

.......................................................................................................................................

...........................................................................................................................................

MONTH | DAY | YEAR

.......................................................................................................................................

...........................................................................................................................................

MONTH | DAY | YEAR

.......................................................................................................................................

...........................................................................................................................................

...........................................................................................................................................

*All moms feel like a failure at some point or another. How have you felt like a #momfail recently (and how much junk food are you eating to cope)?*

When's a time you thought "I got this" and it turned out you didn't have it? What about a time you worried that your kids would melt down and they ended up acting like normal humanoids?

Children are fucking crazy...
Like, at the park, certain
jungle gyms have an opening
for older kids to jump out of.
She's 19 months; she can't
jump. She just walks off it as
if she's on a pirate ship.

—MILA KUNIS, actress and
philanthropist

MONTH | DAY | YEAR

......................................................................................................................

......................................................................................................................

MONTH | DAY | YEAR

......................................................................................................................

......................................................................................................................

MONTH | DAY | YEAR

......................................................................................................................

......................................................................................................................

MONTH | DAY | YEAR

......................................................................................................................

......................................................................................................................

MONTH | DAY | YEAR

......................................................................................................................

......................................................................................................................

MONTH | DAY | YEAR

......................................................................................................................

......................................................................................................................

MONTH | DAY | YEAR

......................................................................................................................

......................................................................................................................

......................................................................................................................

MONTH | DAY | YEAR

MONTH | DAY | YEAR

MONTH | DAY | YEAR

MONTH | DAY | YEAR

MONTH | DAY | YEAR

MONTH | DAY | YEAR

MONTH | DAY | YEAR

*What is something you fantasize about that seems light-years away?*

Becoming a mom to me means that you have accepted that for the next 16 years of your life, you will have a sticky purse.

—NIA VARDALOS, actress

I didn't think I'd have a child before I got married, but hey, it turned out that way and I wouldn't change a thing. I didn't think I'd have dessert before breakfast this morning, but hey, it turned out that way and I wouldn't change a thing.

—MINDY KALING, actress and author

MONTH | DAY | YEAR

MONTH | DAY | YEAR

MONTH | DAY | YEAR

MONTH | DAY | YEAR

MONTH | DAY | YEAR

MONTH | DAY | YEAR

MONTH | DAY | YEAR

MONTH | DAY | YEAR

MONTH | DAY | YEAR

MONTH | DAY | YEAR

MONTH | DAY | YEAR

MONTH | DAY | YEAR

MONTH | DAY | YEAR

MONTH | DAY | YEAR

*Pink glittery Nikes immediately stained with mud.
A pricey Christmas dress instantly ruined by spit-up.
What is one ridiculously impractical "must-have"
item you splurged on for your kids?*

I feel very blessed to have two wonderful,
healthy children who keep me completely
grounded, sane, and throw up on my shoes
just before I go to an awards show just so I
know to keep it real.

—REESE WITHERSPOON, actress and entrepreneur

People very often say to me, "How did you do it? How did you raise a baby and write a book?" and the answer is, I didn't do housework for four years! I'm not Superwoman, and living in squalor, that was the answer.

—J.K. ROWLING, author

MONTH | DAY | YEAR

MONTH | DAY | YEAR

MONTH | DAY | YEAR

MONTH | DAY | YEAR

MONTH | DAY | YEAR

MONTH | DAY | YEAR

MONTH | DAY | YEAR

*"Having it all" is a load of crap because:*

Fist bump to the parents who played musical beds last night and woke up with a swift kick to the kidney under a PJ Masks blanket.

—ME, exhausted mom who co-sleeps against my will

MONTH | DAY | YEAR

.....................................................................................................................

.....................................................................................................................

MONTH | DAY | YEAR

.....................................................................................................................

.....................................................................................................................

MONTH | DAY | YEAR

.....................................................................................................................

.....................................................................................................................

MONTH | DAY | YEAR

.....................................................................................................................

.....................................................................................................................

MONTH | DAY | YEAR

.....................................................................................................................

.....................................................................................................................

MONTH | DAY | YEAR

.....................................................................................................................

.....................................................................................................................

MONTH | DAY | YEAR

.....................................................................................................................

.....................................................................................................................

.....................................................................................................................

MONTH | DAY | YEAR

MONTH | DAY | YEAR

MONTH | DAY | YEAR

MONTH | DAY | YEAR

MONTH | DAY | YEAR

MONTH | DAY | YEAR

MONTH | DAY | YEAR

Only I can understand my kid. she's like "BDIDKDKODKDHJXUDHEJSLOSJDHDUSJMSOZUZUSJSIXOJ" and I'm like "okay I will get you a piece of sausage in just a minute."

—CHRISSY TEIGEN, model and author

When my kids become wild and unruly, I use a nice, safe playpen. When they're finished, I climb out.

—ERMA BOMBECK, humorist and writer

MONTH | DAY | YEAR

MONTH | DAY | YEAR

MONTH | DAY | YEAR

MONTH | DAY | YEAR

MONTH | DAY | YEAR

MONTH | DAY | YEAR

MONTH | DAY | YEAR

MONTH | DAY | YEAR

MONTH | DAY | YEAR

MONTH | DAY | YEAR

MONTH | DAY | YEAR

MONTH | DAY | YEAR

MONTH | DAY | YEAR

MONTH | DAY | YEAR

Like all parents, my husband and I just do the best we can, and hold our breath, and hope we've set aside enough money to pay for our kids' therapy.

—MICHELLE PFEIFFER, actress

*How do you find balance between having a complete shitshow of a house and seeing your kids on Dr. Phil someday versus being a super-organized Pinterest mom whose kids eat organic vegetables and play the cello?*

"Are you fine being hugged while you pee?" is a question someone should've asked me before I had kids.

—KATE CARTIA, writer and creator of *As Kate Would Have It*

MONTH | DAY | YEAR

MONTH | DAY | YEAR

MONTH | DAY | YEAR

MONTH | DAY | YEAR

MONTH | DAY | YEAR

MONTH | DAY | YEAR

MONTH | DAY | YEAR

How do you eke out alone time? Do you get up at the ass-crack of dawn to drink coffee in peace? Or is "alone time" an LOL-worthy and totally alien concept?

If your baby is "beautiful and perfect, never cries or fusses, sleeps on schedule and burps on demand, an angel all the time," you're the grandma.

—TERESA BLOOMINGDALE, author

MONTH | DAY | YEAR

......................................................................................................

......................................................................................................

MONTH | DAY | YEAR

......................................................................................................

......................................................................................................

MONTH | DAY | YEAR

......................................................................................................

......................................................................................................

MONTH | DAY | YEAR

......................................................................................................

......................................................................................................

MONTH | DAY | YEAR

......................................................................................................

......................................................................................................

MONTH | DAY | YEAR

......................................................................................................

......................................................................................................

MONTH | DAY | YEAR

......................................................................................................

......................................................................................................

......................................................................................................

MONTH | DAY | YEAR

MONTH | DAY | YEAR

MONTH | DAY | YEAR

MONTH | DAY | YEAR

MONTH | DAY | YEAR

MONTH | DAY | YEAR

MONTH | DAY | YEAR

*What's the worst thing you found after asking yourself, "What's that smell?"*

She already knows how to drywall because she puts holes in the wall.

—BLAKE LIVELY, actress

I finally discovered something more annoying than my kids... Your kids.

—AMY HUNTER, writer and creator of Outnumbered Mother by Amy Hunter

MONTH | DAY | YEAR

·····································································································

·····································································································

MONTH | DAY | YEAR

·····································································································

·····································································································

MONTH | DAY | YEAR

·····································································································

·····································································································

MONTH | DAY | YEAR

·····································································································

·····································································································

MONTH | DAY | YEAR

·····································································································

·····································································································

MONTH | DAY | YEAR

·····································································································

·····································································································

MONTH | DAY | YEAR

·····································································································

·····································································································

·····································································································

MONTH | DAY | YEAR

····················································································································

····················································································································

MONTH | DAY | YEAR

····················································································································

····················································································································

MONTH | DAY | YEAR

····················································································································

····················································································································

MONTH | DAY | YEAR

····················································································································

····················································································································

MONTH | DAY | YEAR

····················································································································

····················································································································

MONTH | DAY | YEAR

····················································································································

····················································································································

MONTH | DAY | YEAR

····················································································································

····················································································································

····················································································································

The secret to a happy Saturday morning is cuddles and love. Just kidding. It's iPads and high chairs with buckles.

—HOLLY LOFTIN, writer and creator of
From the Bottom of My Purse

How are you seriously kicking ass as a mom? (And how are you mediocre, but totally fine with it?)

If John Lennon was right that life is what happens when you're making other plans, parenthood is what happens when everything is flipped over and spilling everywhere and you can't find a towel or a sponge or your "inside" voice.

— KELLY CORRIGAN, author of *Lift*

MONTH | DAY | YEAR

MONTH | DAY | YEAR

MONTH | DAY | YEAR

MONTH | DAY | YEAR

MONTH | DAY | YEAR

MONTH | DAY | YEAR

MONTH | DAY | YEAR

*What is one thing your kid wrecked so badly that you just threw it away rather than try to salvage it?*

Describe an "Oh, shit. This kid is just like me" moment.

One day I'll be thankful my daughter is an independent, iron-willed human with an unrelenting strong voice, but not today. Not in this grocery store.

—MORGAN MUSIC, writer and creator of House Feminist

MONTH | DAY | YEAR

MONTH | DAY | YEAR

MONTH | DAY | YEAR

MONTH | DAY | YEAR

MONTH | DAY | YEAR

MONTH | DAY | YEAR

MONTH | DAY | YEAR

# END-OF-YEAR REFLECTIONS

## Hurray!

You made it through a year! Time to look back at all the milestones, big and small—like the first time your toddler stayed dry all day in "big-kid" underpants or crept out of bed in the morning, turned on the TV, and let you sleep in. It's those moments, and our unconditional, endless love for our teeny velociraptors that keep us sane (mostly) on the roller-coaster ride that is motherhood.

As you answer these end-of-year prompts, you'll be reminded why *this* is the best and most important job you'll ever do (even if you just scrubbed poop from under your fingernails for the umpteenth time). Take time to realize what a bad-ass mommy you really are (even if you haven't showered in three days and just ate cold chicken nuggets for breakfast), and hopefully you'll feel inspired to pass this journal on to another mom who could use that same reminder.

*What day or moment stands out the most from this past year and why?*

...........................................................................
...........................................................................
...........................................................................
...........................................................................
...........................................................................
...........................................................................
...........................................................................
...........................................................................
...........................................................................

*Describe your biggest WTF DO I DO RIGHT NOW moment this year.*

...........................................................................
...........................................................................
...........................................................................
...........................................................................
...........................................................................
...........................................................................
...........................................................................
...........................................................................
...........................................................................
...........................................................................

*Describe a time you felt your protective mama bear emerge.*

..........................................................................................
..........................................................................................
..........................................................................................
..........................................................................................
..........................................................................................
..........................................................................................
..........................................................................................
..........................................................................................
..........................................................................................

*Describe a time this year when the love you felt for your kids was so overwhelming your heart nearly exploded.*

..........................................................................................
..........................................................................................
..........................................................................................
..........................................................................................
..........................................................................................
..........................................................................................
..........................................................................................
..........................................................................................

*Describe a funny parenting moment from this year that made you laugh so hard you peed a little bit.*

....................................................................

....................................................................

....................................................................

....................................................................

....................................................................

....................................................................

....................................................................

....................................................................

....................................................................

....................................................................

*What is the one thing of which you're most proud during the past 12 months?*

....................................................................

....................................................................

....................................................................

....................................................................

....................................................................

....................................................................

....................................................................

....................................................................

....................................................................

....................................................................

*And what is one thing you regret and wish you could go back and redo?*

*What was the biggest shocker of this past year?*

*If you could say one thing to yourself one year ago, what would it be?*

........................................................................

........................................................................

........................................................................

........................................................................

........................................................................

........................................................................

........................................................................

........................................................................

........................................................................

*What is something you know you could never have survived without this past year?*

........................................................................

........................................................................

........................................................................

........................................................................

........................................................................

........................................................................

........................................................................

........................................................................

........................................................................

........................................................................

*If you were to write your child(ren) a letter today, what would you tell them?*

*What are you grateful for?*

..................................................................................................................................

..................................................................................................................................

..................................................................................................................................

..................................................................................................................................

..................................................................................................................................

..................................................................................................................................

..................................................................................................................................

..................................................................................................................................

..................................................................................................................................

*What are you still a little bit pissed about?*

..................................................................................................................................

..................................................................................................................................

..................................................................................................................................

..................................................................................................................................

..................................................................................................................................

..................................................................................................................................

..................................................................................................................................

..................................................................................................................................

..................................................................................................................................

*Who has been your biggest cheerleader on this journey? What made this person so supportive?*

..................................................................

..................................................................

..................................................................

..................................................................

..................................................................

..................................................................

..................................................................

..................................................................

..................................................................

..................................................................

*What's the best, truest piece of advice or wisdom you received about raising kids?*

..................................................................

..................................................................

..................................................................

..................................................................

..................................................................

..................................................................

..................................................................

..................................................................

..................................................................

..................................................................

Now that you're a bit more of a "seasoned" mom, what is one piece of advice you'd give to a mom-to-be?

*What would you say today to a sanctimommy passing judgment on you (or another mom)?*

...................................................................
...................................................................
...................................................................
...................................................................
...................................................................
...................................................................
...................................................................
...................................................................
...................................................................
...................................................................

*In what way(s) are you exactly the mom you expected you'd be?*

...................................................................
...................................................................
...................................................................
...................................................................
...................................................................
...................................................................
...................................................................
...................................................................
...................................................................
...................................................................
...................................................................

*And in what way(s) are you nothing like the mom you expected yourself to be?*

..............................................................................
..............................................................................
..............................................................................
..............................................................................
..............................................................................
..............................................................................
..............................................................................
..............................................................................
..............................................................................

*Motherhood is:*

..............................................................................
..............................................................................
..............................................................................
..............................................................................
..............................................................................
..............................................................................
..............................................................................
..............................................................................
..............................................................................
..............................................................................
..............................................................................

# CONGRATULATIONS!

[ Your Picture Here ]

you kept it together!*

*mostly

## ABOUT THE AUTHOR

Known on the Internet as The 21st Century SAHM (and at home as Mommyyyyyy!! and Moooooom!!), **KAREN JOHNSON** is a former English teacher, turned stay-at-home mom, turned writer on all things parenthood—some funny, some heartfelt. Karen is a staff writer and social media manager for *Scary Mommy* and an assistant editor for *Sammiches and Psych Meds*. Her writing can also be found on her own site, *The 21st Century SAHM* (the21st centurysahm.com), on other parenting and family websites such as *Her View from Home* and *Babble*, and in several anthologies. In her free time (haha, yeah right) she enjoys traveling with her family, reading, exercising, and then undoing her entire workout by drinking beer and eating pizza.

## ABOUT THE ILLUSTRATOR

**CHELSEA LARSSON** is an illustrator by night, a UX writer by day, and a mom all the time. She lives in Berkeley, California, with her husband and two-year-old daughter. She's mostly got it together, except for when her daughter is hangry. Or when she is hangry. Basically, snacks are the only thing keeping her family intact. Her work has been in *Bravery* magazine and *Illustoria* magazine, and she's the creator of *Life is Boobiful*, a zine about breastfeeding.

CPSIA information can be obtained
at www.ICGtesting.com
Printed in the USA
LVHW051704110719
623812LV00006B/9/P